Conversations in Spirit

by

John Allan

Letitia Caron

Caroline Terrell

DeVorss & Company
P.O. Box 550
Marina del Rey, California 90291

07/09

Copyright © 1981
by John Allan, Letitia Caron, Caroline Terrell

All Rights Reserved

ISBN: 0-87516-452-8
Library of Congress Card Catalog No: 81-66244

Printed in the United States of America
by Book Graphics, Inc., California

Contents

Conversations in Spirit

I

How We Experience Spirit

JOHN: I think before we can answer this question of how we experience Spirit, we must first define what we mean by Spirit. We realize the difficulty in attempting to define something that's outside the limits of the human mind and senses. Therefore, rather than trying to define verbally what Spirit is, perhaps it will help to describe what Spirit feels like. For Spirit can definitely be felt.

For me Spirit is felt in two distinct ways. First, It's felt as a sense of joy, love and harmony which permeates and replaces those feelings of the mind and senses. Many people, I'm sure, have felt at least an intimation of Spirit, as they've walked the beach, or strolled the woods, or have looked up at the stars on a clear summer's night. The joyous sense of peace, the gentle loving freedom and harmony with everything about is close to, if not the actual sensing of Spirit.

Second, there's a sensing of the power of Spirit— a power so great that, at times, it stuns the body and makes it almost immobile. This feeling of Spirit's power is simply the growth and deepening of Spirit's love. It is one of the most dynamic, beautiful and absolute experiences that we've ever found, especially when the power is so great that it fills us. When this happens we don't exist as body and mind. Rather, we feel ourselves as a new entity. A pure being. One connected totally to God. And in this connection with God we feel a sense of timelessness which is our participation with God's eternity.

Would you say that this has explained how Spirit feels?

CAROLINE AND LETITIA: Yes.

JOHN: We must remember that the explanation is not the actual experiencing of Spirit; also that there are many gradations and intensities of experiencing Spirit found between these two poles.

Having said this, perhaps now we can ask how can one begin to sense Spirit? For certainly many people may wish to experience Spirit's energy, and through such experiencing have their lives transformed. So I think it will help if each one of us explains how we first sensed Spirit.

Our First Experiencing of Spirit

LETITIA: I remember prior to feeling Spirit in fullness, I had been searching for God for quite some time. It hadn't become a desperate search, because ever since I was a child I had always believed in God. But now I wanted my faith to give me a direction. And it wasn't. All I really knew, or thought I knew about God was what I'd been taught. So I started to explore other ideas about God. I began reading books of both eastern and western religions. I listened more closely when people would bring up the subject of "God." In addition to this I began praying more often, not just out of need, but out of the desire to be close to God. I set aside some time every day to read some religious work that might inspire me. I remember one article I had read said that I could hear God's voice if I were to remain still enough to listen. I learned Thai Chi and practiced it many times a day. And through these methods I started feeling that there was more to my life than I had experienced by worshipping God in a more traditional manner.

But even as good as I sometimes felt by doing these things, after a while these methods didn't work anymore. Many times when trying to meditate, I would feel frustrated because I knew it had become a ritual and was insincere.

During this time I was told by a religious teacher that everyone must come as close as possible to God in this life in order to progress toward God in the next life. It sounded reasonable. But again I was being filled with everyone's opinion on how to evolve spiritually. Everyone was telling me how to find "the way" and I just didn't believe it anymore. I had reached a dead end. Nothing had brought me close to God.

One morning, around this time, I was sitting on a hilltop trying to meditate with an inspirational book. Getting nowhere, I threw the book down. I felt empty and disgusted. From this deep sense of discouragement, I began to recall John's and my discussion a few days before about the possibility of feeling God's energy. Not knowing whether I could or not, I prayed, "God what is true? Can I feel You? If so, what do I have to learn before I can?"

With this prayer came the question of whether I had ever felt God before. At that moment I felt a release. I felt for the first time I could be honest with myself. I could forget all the things I had been told because they hadn't really helped me.

Within a few days after this experience, I saw John again. This time I was more open to what he was saying. I also saw that he was the first person who didn't give me a method or discipline to follow. Nor did he give me his personal ideas of who or what God was or how we could be more God centered. He again merely suggested the possibility of feeling the energy of God's Spirit. And he told me how he felt the energy.

As we talked through the course of the evening the sensing of Spirit's love began to grow stronger and stronger as if building upon itself. And as it did, joy just flooded into me. The feeling was totally unrelated to anything I had read or believed or had been told about God. It was whole and complete, like nothing but God could be. Thank you, Father.

Looking back on that experience, I realize I had to some degree experienced God's love and joy before without ever identifying it. I believe many people feel God's love at moments in their lives. This might be the reason so many people believe in God without ever really living with Him.

JOHN: Because they have sensed Spirit's energy on occasion.

CAROLINE: Yes, I had sensed this love a few times, too, but I hadn't connected it with God. The first experience I remember came when I was in analysis. When I sensed this beautiful love I thought it was because I was O.K.—O.K. psychologically.

JOHN: You mean you first sensed Spirit during psychotherapy sessions?

CAROLINE: Not in the office, but sometimes at home. I remember once I felt this sense when I saw a shaft of sunlight coming across an oakwood floor. I was walking into my house. There was such love. It was so beautiful. But I don't think I felt it for more than two seconds. And I thought, "Wow, I must really be in tune today. I must really be clear."

JOHN: Do you recall what led up to that experience?

CAROLINE: About that time my husband and I were going through a separation and I couldn't make the payments on the house my children and I were living in. After several months of struggle and worry, I found I couldn't solve my problem. So I just gave up and called on God to help me.

I remember I felt like a plane going through a sound barrier. I just broke through into absolute

5

peace. It suddenly didn't bother me that the bills were there, and that I was going to lose the house. It just didn't bother me. And I never did understand that until later when it occurred to me that God may have helped me. But I didn't connect these things with God at that time.

And then another time, after I had been on my own for awhile, I really became frightened about taking care of my children and trying to bring in enough money. So I called on God again, not really believing in a sense. Not knowing whether I would be answered.

I remember putting a whole stack of bills in a little paper sack and writing on the outside of the sack, ''God, you'll have to help me pay these, I can't.'' And then I put them in my desk and closed the drawer. I guess it was several weeks later that seven hundred dollars came in. And it was almost exactly what I needed. Once again I didn't connect it with God because I wasn't living a life focused on Spirit.

JOHN: You didn't connect it? Or did you connect it only for a moment, and then it was forgotten?

CAROLINE: I think I realized God had helped me when the money came in, but I didn't realize the significance of it. God wasn't real enough to me. I only called upon Him in times of desperation.

Also at that time I wasn't really searching for God—I was just trying to find happiness.

JOHN: The point that I first experienced Spirit was

similar to both of yours. I too felt down and discouraged—at the end of my rope, so to speak. My problems centered on feelings of self doubt and the meaninglessness of life.

I remember in college when I studied philosophy and psychology my whole conservative religious upbringing was uprooted and I was thrown into a state of confusion and anxiety. I felt unanchored. I felt my life had little meaning. In a word I was miserable. Life seemed hopeless.

Later, when I got married, I was constantly fretting about how I was going to support a wife and a child who was on the way. I was worried whether I could make a success in business. The horrible self doubts that constantly hounded me were horrendous and interfered with many of my human relationships.

Then one night I was alone in the house. I remember I laid my newspaper down and turned out the light. I put my head back and tried to relax. But all the thoughts of my struggles and fears descended on me like an avalanche. In the midst of my anguish I cried out and said, "God, if You're there please show me."

With these words the rush of thoughts began to diminish. After a while my mind became quite clear. And then I began to feel as if I were being lifted up and suspended in air. I don't know how long this feeling lasted, perhaps two or three minutes. . . . and then it began to happen. It was as if a large veil parted before me. And there stood another veil which also opened. And a third did the same. Now the veils were opening faster. And I was moving more quickly through them. This is how it felt, as if I was passing through these veils. Finally I saw there was only one more veil and as this opened I was free. I was within the space of an infinite universe.

The movement still went on. I was being drawn deeper into the infinitude of this space where no object existed. Not an object was there. None was needed. For It, this Perfection of Love, was totally whole and needed no objects for Its wholeness and perfection.

The awesomeness of the experience was overwhelming. Suddenly I became frightened. I drew back, shook my head, and opened my eyes. The space was gone. The experience had ended. But its love and joy remained. In fact, it was fully two weeks before I came down from that magnificent plateau created by the experience. During that time my fears and doubts diminished. And I felt a peace I'd never known before.

That experience with its love and joy and freedom was what began my search for God. Today I know that it was God who answered my plea that night. And it is He who has guided me ever since. I've never again experienced Spirit exactly that way. For this kind of experience probably hasn't been needed.

I think by describing our first experiences with Spirit we see better what triggered the experience. First we were all feeling a sense of despair. At that time we turned to God and asked Him for help. And that's when He began to reveal Himself to us.

This "revealing" or discovering that there really is a God, I believe, can be experienced by everyone. When we are ready and willing to drop our ego-centered lives for a moment, and open ourselves to His life completely, God will always allow us to participate with His Spirit.

This dropping of my ego-centered life took me a long time to fully experience. For after my initial experiencing of Spirit, it was years before I again felt Spirit to any great degree. I remember during this time how I searched through eastern religions, western psychology, mysticism and about every other philosophy, psychology and religion I could find. But it did no good. The re-experiencing of God seemed even further away after all this searching.

Then, one day, feeling deeply discouraged and frustrated, I thought back on my first experiencing of God. It occurred to me the experience had happened without my doing anything. Through all my present search I was always doing something. I was meditating, quieting the mind, being open to God, waiting for the opening of an inner eye, and so on.

So where the original experience had just happened, my present seeking involved intense human effort which created an enlargement and focus on self.

"But how do I *not* make an effort to find God?" I asked, which I found wasn't really the point. For trying not to make an effort can be a greater effort than making an effort.

So after all these mental maneuverings I finally came to the realization that to make an effort or not to make an effort to find God was not the question. Rather, the truth of the matter was, *I couldn't find God. I didn't the first time and I couldn't now. And how could I expect to, with this finite mechanism called a mind, which studied and practiced techniques of quieting itself, expanding itself, extinguishing itself—endlessly trying to do something with itself.*

And that's when the realization was born of yielding or dropping self. The yielding or dropping of all effort or non-effort. The yielding or dropping of all attempts to find God through any method.

Along with this realization came the understanding of what humility really meant. Humility was not a concept or a state of mind that could be cultivated. Humility was the deep realization that one doesn't know either about this human life, because it's so changeable, enigmatic and illusory; nor about God's life, because though Spirit can be felt, God's Being is beyond all human knowing—His qualities are so perfect, pure and untouched by this world that they're beyond all definition, categorization or comparison.

When you realize deeply that you don't know, it becomes so much easier to drop self and yield to God. For pride of self is no longer resisting such yielding.

So for the next several years, when I did come to that point of spontaneously dropping and yielding self, I began to experience God's energy. There were many joyous episodes of His life beginning again to replace my fears and self doubts, and my daily concerns over money, business and the safety and well being of my family.

10

With this experiencing of God's energy the mystical concepts I'd gathered over the years began to fade away—by that I mean my desires to achieve visionary, clairvoyant, out-of-body experiences which many esoteric philosophies that I had been studying had encouraged. I began to realize that all these experiences had little to do with the energy of love that I was now experiencing from God.

The Difference Between Psychic Energy and Spirit's Energy

JOHN: After feeling God's Spirit, we realize there's a vast difference between psychic energy and the energy of Spirit. Without discerning the difference between the two, a person can become tremendously confused and get forever side-tracked in his search for God.

As we've found, psychic energy is concerned with and dependent on the mind—either the mind's projections, the mind's extrasensory experiences or the mind's receptivity to esoteric vibrations and mental forces occurring from within and from without. So we see that with psychic energy the mind is always involved either actively or passively.

The energy of God is experienced entirely differently. The mind is not involved with the generating or receiving of Spirit's energy. In fact the mind must, at least partially, be out of the way, dropped, in a state of yielding, before Spirit's energy can be felt.

So the question arises, if the mind—and by that I mean also the senses which are part of the mind—doesn't feel Spirit, what does? I believe, when we are temporarily out of the way that what we begin to feel is Spirit Itself. In other words when we're not there for a moment, then what is eternally there, Spirit, becomes evident. At that moment we then, to some extent, begin to participate in God's Beingness. We begin to feel the way Spirit feels Itself!

CAROLINE: A lot of times when you feel psychic energy you assume it's from God because it is an energy. But this energy does not bring about satisfaction in your search for God. You still search hoping that the next new psychic discovery through the next new book will reveal God to you.

Once you feel God's energy there's no question of its Source. The search to find Him is ended. Now you can let Him teach you about Himself.

LETITIA: When one feels the energy of God there can be no confusion with psychic energy.

CAROLINE: For a long time I was caught in the psychic and metaphysical fields. So I understand how many people feel. I thought I'd find God somehow through learning about my past lives; through out-of-body experiences; through E.S.P., or whatever. All these things were intriguing and mysterious to me because I thought they would take me a step higher. I felt if I could just sort them out, I'd finally understand who God was. I believed I was on the "path." I even felt that being able to "read" the future was part of my growth.

I admired very much a friend of mine because she was clairvoyant. When I asked her how she could foretell the future, she said, "Well, I think it's the Holy Spirit that speaks to me." That was her version of what she believed the Holy Spirit to be. So I prayed to receive the Holy Spirit thinking it would make me clairvoyant, too.

When I did experience Spirit It was entirely different from anything I had ever felt. It had nothing to do with psychicness or clairvoyance, or what I believed the Holy Spirit to be. It felt entirely different from any psychic experience I'd ever had. In fact, Spirit took away all my desire to be involved any longer in the psychic field.

When I actually experienced Spirit fully and deeply, it was in response to a healing I was receiving for my back. I had been in a car accident and my back had been giving me pain for weeks. It hurt terribly. Lying down, sitting up, standing, nothing helped. There was no relief from the pain. I went to a chiropractor several times and he couldn't find anything wrong. I went to a medical doctor and he couldn't find anything wrong, either. He recommended a neurosurgeon for me to see.

After I left the doctor's office I started to drive over to see the neurosurgeon, but I just couldn't go. Something else had been crossing my mind. A friend of mine knew someone who had brought healings to people. She had introduced this man named John to me and I had felt an instant trust in him. I had never thought before of being healed by anyone other than a doctor, but this time it felt right. So that same day I asked John for help.

Later that evening as I was standing at the kitchen sink washing the dinner dishes, this tremendous love began to come through me. I'll never forget that. It was all through the room and all through me. It felt like a presence there of dear, all-encompassing love. And my back just went into place like an old creaky ship. There was a gentle sensation of love adjusting my back and putting it into place.

And that's how Spirit first came fully to me. The experience was so strong and deep and full of our Father's love that my life changed from that moment on.

The Meaning of Directing

JOHN: People have asked me how these healings occur. As with your healing, Caroline, the first thing I do is get John Allan out of the way. Then when there's no blockage from self, I can powerfully and confidently direct the energy of God to the person in need.

It's really simple. But the person who's receiving the energy should be open to receive it. Otherwise it could pass them by. In other words, they must attempt to be quiet with an open expectancy so that they can feel the directing.

14

You know, it's fairly easy to be open to Spirit when you're sick and want to be healed, for you want to be out of your misery. But to be open to Spirit at other times is quite difficult because our many human involvements interfere and we become committed.

I believe it's only the uncommitted who will be continuously seeking for God. By uncommitted I mean those who put their life with God first and everything else second. For the person who puts his human commitments first is signifying by his actions that these are primary in his life. Thus his life with God will naturally be secondary.

Commitment can take many different forms. One of the more subtle forms is one's commitment to religious beliefs rather than God.

I remember not too long ago, a friend of mine and I sat on my front porch having lunch. For several hours we talked about Spirit. All the while I was directing the energy toward him. But he wasn't receiving it because of his commitment to his religious beliefs. Every time I'd talk about how Spirit could heal and transform one's life he'd respond with, "Well, yes, you're right, John, all you have to do is really claim these things—claim God's Spirit and Its benefits as one's own." And I thought, "Oh dear, there's no way Spirit is ever going to break through these beliefs and ideas." The interesting thing was later his beliefs did break down, because they didn't satisfy him. Then, because of his strong desire for God, he did begin to feel Spirit.

15

LETITIA: He was probably primed for the feeling and recognition of Spirit. And then when one brings Spirit to the primed person he begins to feel It.

JOHN: Exactly.

CAROLINE: And it doesn't have to be an obvious priming. Somehow it seems that God is preparing us without our knowing it.

LETITIA: We're only realizing this now. We didn't consciously know we were being prepared at the time.

JOHN: That's right.

Some Problems With Meditation

CAROLINE: I was wondering about people who meditate until their minds are still. It seems that would be a kind of priming. If your mind can be completely silent and you're desiring God, then you would be almost in a state of openness or of being able to receive. How could a mind be so quiet and clear and not be open to God? Or is it?

JOHN: I think many times there is a sincere desire behind the attempt to find God through the stilling of the mind. Many people see that as long as the mind is constantly active there's no space left for God. So they set about trying to find a sense of quiet with the hope that God or Truth will be there. I feel a lot of well-meaning people have thought this way.

I know in my search for God, I read many writers who said that the reason for unhappiness, anxiety, distress was the mind. Therefore the answer was to quiet the mind. And I said, "Yes, that's right. It's logical if the mind's the problem and I can silence the mind then I'm done with the problem." So I sought for years and years to try to silence the mind with the idea of not only solving my problems, but also of finding God in the silence.

LETITIA: God is not something that can be attained. God is not an attainment. When you seek to attain Spirit through any self-conscious means It's always gone. It's never there.

JOHN: We can't attain God. We can only participate with God.

CAROLINE: You're always working against what He can give you when you try to attain God. I think that's one of the problems when you first come into Spirit—trying to attain the same feeling that you had the day before. You don't know at first that Spirit is given in different ways according to our needs.

JOHN: Another problem in attempting to attain God through stilling the mind is the tremendous amount of effort attached to this endeavor.

A popular form of meditation attempts to merge the mind with the object of one's meditation. The goal is commendable, for when such a merging does happen one is in a state of union with everything about, which surely has the fragrance of Love—of

17

Spirit. But the effort in making the mental break-through is tremendous and such effort can lead to frustration, hardness and excessive self-will.

Also, as I found, even when I had "merged" my mind with the tree or flower or whatever, there may have been no movement in the mind, but many times there was no God, either.

CAROLINE: It's because one may be focusing on the effort and techniques. The same thing can happen when one focuses on the effort to yield to God.

LETITIA: This could be helpful to someone who might be experiencing blocks in his meditation.

JOHN: And if one doesn't overcome these blocks then the search for God becomes extremely difficult.

LETITIA: I wonder if in our search for God we receive what we're seeking?

JOHN: I don't think we do.

LETITIA: Because what we really thought we were searching for was not what we received.

JOHN: Exactly. I know I thought God was a void, a state of emptiness, a state of stillness, because that's what I'd been told by "experts" on these matters. Therefore I practiced meditation according to these concepts. When God did become evident, I saw this wasn't the truth at all. The truth is that God is a God of Spirit and Love.

CAROLINE: That seems to be the problem in meditation. The goal has already been given. And one may believe that the goal reached *is* God. It seems, we are always telling God who He is instead of letting *God* tell us who He is.

It's good to have the mind stilled, but if the belief is that stillness is God then you've missed it. You haven't given yourself a chance to receive what God would give you.

JOHN: The interesting thing is that the god you find with an absolutely still mind is not always the God which comes to you when you have relinquished self. Because the former is working from the standpoint of the mind. And even when the mind is still, it's still the mind being still. And therefore what that mind finds at the end of its stillness is not necessarily God.

CAROLINE: The mind has found the concept of a still mind.

JOHN: And the end of the still mind's quest is a state of stillness or emptiness, which many of us believe to be God.

CAROLINE: Which is peace from the world. Therefore one thinks one's found God. Instead of finding Spirit, which gradually converts the world into heaven for you, you've found times of stillness and peace— a welcome relief from the world—but it is not the fullness of life that Spirit brings.

LETITIA: That is so true because one doesn't know that he can live a different life. He only feels he can be free of the world's noise and problems for a few moments or hours.

CAROLINE: The ultimate would be to find a retreat to avoid the problems of the world.

Other Concepts of God

LETITIA: I didn't think of God as being some emptiness or void because I'd never been taught in those terms. I thought of God as an entity possessing the qualities that Jesus had. I didn't think Jesus was God. But I thought that the good qualities that were in him were of God. And through experiencing those qualities, feeling those qualities, living with those qualities, that would be finding God.

CAROLINE: I think for many of us Jesus is the only concept given us about God.

LETITIA: Yes. Because he's referred to as the Son of God.

JOHN: And as he once supposedly said to a disciple, "He that hath seen me hath seen the Father." This could lead one into believing that Jesus was God. But when you once feel Spirit you realize the infinitude of Spirit is far greater than any one person.

CAROLINE: My concepts of God were that He was beyond understanding and so vast that He was unreachable. That's why I didn't recognize Spirit when I first felt It. Perhaps it was that the human sense of me was not recognizing the Spirit sense of me that had come forth. Perhaps that is what "reborn" means; the truth of you as Spirit dissolving away the sense of you as material.

LETITIA: What did you believe that God was?

CAROLINE: I really don't know. I do know that I didn't believe what I was taught in church about God's punishing us. I never could equate that with God. It just didn't make sense, even though a friend of mine a number of years ago tried to convince me that God, being whole and perfect, is therefore a combination of positive and negative.

LETITIA: I know a lot of people say that the negative that happens is really positive, but we can't understand why because we're not advanced enough.

JOHN: We've all heard people say that God allows sickness, accident and death to occur. It's all part of His marvelous plan. This is a terrible denigration of Spirit's caring and love, and absolute goodness.

CAROLINE: I remember the Bible states that the Lord giveth and taketh away, which reflects so many peoples' reasoning regarding death. But I think a deeper meaning is that the Lord gives good and takes away evil. That's what Spirit teaches. It gives us life and takes away death.

JOHN: But you really have to die to that false sense of self while you're here on earth to know this.

CAROLINE: Yes. When you begin to feel Spirit, you begin to die to the false concept of who you are. Then you begin to come alive as to who you really are with Spirit. And you come to realize that, in a sense, you've been going through a process of death; death to a false sense of yourself and alive to a true sense of yourself.

JOHN: Yes, death to a time-based sense of your life, and alive to the eternal sense of your life with God.

LETITIA: And in the deepening of your life with Spirit you begin to feel the body as a part of this being with God.

CAROLINE: The body has been transformed into being.

JOHN: We should remember that we're describing different aspects of our participation with God's Spirit, which converts our sense of human life into a sense of a life with Spirit.

LETITIA: Yes, a sense of being filled with love. That's what God feels like to me. A sense of beautiful love.

Recently I had a conversation with a gentleman who was ill. I asked him if he felt God was a God of love. He responded, "Not necessarily." He said he had prayed for his sick brother and his brother had died despite his prayers. That's when he decided that God did things according to whim. "God saves lives, but He also takes lives," he stated. "Therefore when it's my time then God will take me." He had no idea that God could be a loving sense that he could feel. Absolutely none. I think a lot of people feel this way.

JOHN: Until one experiences God's energy one can't realize that God is absolute love. Because this man prayed and his prayers hadn't been answered, he considered God to be a God of judgment and retribution.

Why Some Prayers Aren't Answered

CAROLINE: This situation of people praying for another person's life is happening thousands of times every day. And while there are many healings taking place, there are also many of those being prayed for who die. Why?

JOHN: I believe the major reason is the false assumptions we have about ourselves. Feeling ourselves as physical, and deeming ourselves as a person or soul living within the confines of a physical body, we arrive at false conclusions regarding what constitutes life and what causes death. We feel that life is in the body and death occurs when the body loses its life. And upon these conclusions all our medical theories are developed, all our beliefs are based, all our fears are formed. For if the body is the basis of our life then when the body dies our life is done, notwithstanding the many theories about reincarnation, or the soul going to heaven.

So we see that if we pray for a person believing he's only a body, seeing him only as a body, feeling that his only life is contained within the body, then our prayers will be filled with fear and doubt. For it's evident how vulnerable and susceptible the body is to all the human laws associated with accident, disease and death.

But if through feeling our connection with God we begin to see our real identity, one that is of Spirit, then we can begin to see who everyone truly is. And from this base we can pray so much more effectively, because so many of our false concepts have dropped away, which diminishes our fears. Therefore the potency of our prayers will have increased tremendously.

CAROLINE: When we pray for others in what seems like a life and death situation, we should realize that God can *only* give life. His life.

LETITIA: It seems that if the person praying for a healing gets too focused on the outcome then he is not focused on his connection with God. Or on the love he feels from God. This can keep one from receiving the love that's coming from God that can heal his circumstance.

JOHN: We have an idea of the outcome of how we want the healing to occur. Which is natural. But this can also be a block. God will bring the right solution at the right time if we persist in praying for His help, persist in directing His energy, and persist in asking Him to teach us what we need to know to effect a healing.

LETITIA: When we pray for someone, we're working not only to remove the problem, but we're also working for that person to have a connection with Spirit. Spirit *is* life. Therefore Spirit will give him life and restore him to health.

Many times people pray for their life to be given back in the way it was before. But does God give human life back? Could He ever take it away?

CAROLINE: He never gave human life in the first place.

JOHN: He's not going to take it away in the second place.

LETITIA: So the person praying isn't destroying the element that's creating the problem, which is the feeling of being separate from Spirit. And he's not getting in connection with God enough to. . . .

CAROLINE: . . . feel His answer.

LETITIA: And to experience the destruction of the problem.

JOHN: The bottom line, it seems, is what Jesus said, "Thy will be done, Father," knowing that the will of the Father is always goodness and health. It's always life.

That's the simplest of all prayers. And a potent one. Because in any healing we don't know what's best for the person. The Father does but we don't. We know that He only gives life, health and will bring untold blessings to the person.

25

LETITIA: It's important that we relinquish our concepts and ideas of how God should touch our lives or how He should work in our lives. When we can relinquish those ideas for even a moment, and say, "I don't know," then possibly we can be open to receive His answers.

JOHN: Perhaps that's the essence of prayer, to say, "Father, I don't know, please teach me. Bring your Spirit to bear on my sickness, my fears, my problems. Let me feel your Spirit within me."

CAROLINE: How beautiful to know you don't know.

JOHN: What we do realize is that God doesn't allow, ordain or produce sickness, accidents, death or any other adverse circumstance. We realize this from feeling His Spirit. From this participating with Him we find contained within His energy only love, peace, goodness, health, eternal life. Therefore if adverse events happen in our lives we know that God had nothing to do with them. They weren't in any way His will. This can be stated unequivocally.

LETITIA: When one is familiar with the feeling of Spirit and Its absolute love, then one realizes God doesn't allow death. One begins to realize it's the lack of contact between God and those who feel they are dying that allows death to occur. God does not create this separation—fear does. If death does occur it's because fear is a much stronger influence at that moment than the sense of God. And when fear is this strong chances are God is not felt at all. This is why removing fear is an extremely important factor in healing. Perhaps the most important.

JOHN: I was thinking this morning how often we divide life into either Spirit or matter. I remember a statement I made in *The Kingdom of God,* which I now would alter somewhat. I said, in effect, that if you realize your spiritual perfection through feeling Spirit's energy then this realization of perfection would manifest in the physical world.

On one level this is true. But the greater truth is that when one stays constantly deep with Spirit, then one sees no division between a spiritual world and a physical world. There becomes, to one's realization, only a spiritual world. And in this world is all health. All life. All love. So the desire to see anything manifest on the physical level stops. Because one sees, feels, realizes that there really is no physical level. There's only Spirit.

The Meaning of Letting Go

JOHN: So we see that whether we're praying for the healing of others, or praying to receive Spirit, or praying about other concerns, our primary need is to feel God's Spirit—His energy. For without feeling It, we'll never be quite sure that we're near to His love, close to His life, part of His power.

The most effective thing I can do to feel Spirit's energy is to let go. We've all heard this statement before. Religious people have said it for centuries.

27

But if letting go were so easy, then many people would be living with Spirit.

To me letting go means the draining away of all self-conscious thoughts, desires, concerns, responses and tensions within the mind and body.

As you know, each morning I walk the hills around my home "working" for others and myself. Before I can work powerfully for others I have to first make sure I'm fully participating with Spirit's energy. To do this I must drop all that makes up the person called John Allan. For if I'm filled with my concerns, my thoughts, my desires, my bodily tensions, then it's evident there's too much of me and not enough room left to feel the power of God.

I feel it's especially important to let go of the body—release all its internal tensions and sensations. For the body's self-conscious tensions and sensations are the antithesis to the feeling of Spirit. I look at the body as an isolation booth where most of us live encapsuled all of our days. So to "drop" the body is to gain a sense of freedom from this self-enclosure. This can allow us to begin to sense the energy of Spirit that has been blocked off by the bodily senses.

Immediately upon letting go of both body and mind, I begin to feel a great increase in God's power. And as I allow this sense to grow, it becomes so powerful at times, that it seems to propel my legs and animate my body. It begins to permeate my whole being and go beyond.

These are times that it feels as if I've gone through a door of human life and have entered a domain of a life of Spirit. All conscious mental and bodily activity have been left behind. God's energy is now in total command. I sense God's beauty totally. Now I truly have a different life—a life that I'm not managing in the least.

The other evening, Letitia, as we were talking, it happened again. I came to that place of totally letting go. God really took over. For several hours I had no sense of ego or body. No sense of human thought or effort. God did everything for me. At that point He was everything.

LETITIA: I've found, too, that if the body is tense it's almost impossible to be aware of the activity of thought. Before one can see this distracting mental activity, the body must be quiet. Then the hyperenergy of the mind becomes evident.

Before letting go of the body, both body and mind are mixed up together. After letting go of the body, my thoughts can then become quiet through prayer —a gentle prayer saying that "I wish to be with you, Father."

Sometimes the energy of Spirit gently calms me down. It's a very comfortable feeling of peace and love—a feeling one can walk with, or sit with, or pray with, or even share with another. Other times there seems to be a much more dramatic transition. At these times a beautiful understanding may come. A problem might be solved. Or Spirit may be felt as a bursting forth into a fullness of God's love.

JOHN: Beautiful. "A bursting forth into a fullness of God's love." I like that. It really seems that way sometimes. It seems as if we're transported from a world of conscious human activity, sensation, and thought, and taken into another dimension where God simply is. Where His fullness is. And there is no longer any conscious activity of having to do anything. He is just there.

LETITIA AND CAROLINE: Yes.

CAROLINE: There is nothing I can add. I recognize it and listen with joy, and just love it.

Silence

How the Deepening of Spirit Occurs

CAROLINE: Sometimes in the deepening of Spirit comes the feeling that forever I can be this way. There is nothing in the world that I need. I could just stay here forever and be full with Spirit. That's how it feels when it's really full.

LETITIA: Spirit is complete in Itself.

CAROLINE: That's right.

JOHN: Is it the removal of mental and physical obstacles and problems that allows such deepening to occur?

LETITIA: Yes, I think it is. If I feel unable to let go deeply into Spirit for any reason, I will often pray to God for the understanding and release of the resistance.

In my prayer I usually come to the realization that God is the only importance in my life. And I'm living this life because God is giving me His life, and showing me how to give His life to others. From this realization that God *is* my life, Spirit will many times deepen to that fuller sense that we've described.

Another beautiful way of allowing God's life to deepen within me is by directing the energy to myself. Many times, after doing this, I feel nothing but the energy of Spirit everywhere.

CAROLINE: I think, too, it's important for the deepening of Spirit to give God priority the moment we awake. When I wake up I first see how my body feels, which really shows where I am mentally, and how perhaps I've been "worked" mentally through dreams during the night. If I find the body unrested and tense then I begin to let go to allow Spirit to remove that sense of tiredness and tension.

Later as I eat breakfast, I thank God for my life with Him, and sense His love as much as I can allow. After the family has left the house, I usually sit down and work for others. My mornings are geared to going to the hills and that's when I really start feeling close to God. That's my time. My complete opening up to His life. It is my freedom and my time with Him in the deepest sense. The love just grows deeper and deeper as I drive along. It's almost a meditation.

JOHN: It seems from what you're saying, that from the time you wake up in the morning your life is a prayer.

CAROLINE: Yes, it's just beautiful for me.

But sometimes thought will suggest that I can't

31

sense God's Spirit deeply. And then it becomes a constant prayer saying, "Please teach me, Father, to yield more to you."

JOHN: And I think that's important to bring out. There's a learning process that goes on. We learn through familiarity with Spirit, that we must let go for Spirit to be deeply felt. This learning is invaluable, and comes only after repeatedly feeling God's energy. We learn from this familiarity that if we are holding on, then the energy will not be greatly felt.

So to let go is the central lesson we learn. Without this learning we have little hope of living with God deeply and in continuity. Before learning how to let go I was haunted by constant frustration and fear of being without God's energy. One day the energy of Spirit would be sensed intensely and the next day I didn't feel it at all. And when I didn't feel it, fear would intimate, "You'll never have it again."

CAROLINE: Yes, fear is how negative energy has tried to reach me to keep me from living continuously with God. So many times just as I would begin to feel beautifully close to our Father, fear would say to me, "I'm going to disrupt this." It would say, "I can take this closeness away from you."

The beginning of the destruction of this fear happened one day when I was driving up into the hills and was beginning to feel my connection with God. A repetitive thought began to suggest, "I can take it away." I started to pray and almost immediately the realization came that God's life was my life. And a thought could not take away God's life. That was a ridiculous suggestion. So after that occurrence fear of losing that closeness to God never had that much power over me.

LETITIA: Fear of not feeling Spirit seems to be one of the greatest obstacles to Spirit. But there comes the day when you are able to say, "I'm not going to accept this, because the power I feel from God is stronger than fear."

Negative Energy

JOHN: This seems to be the time to bring up the matter of negative energy. I feel it's most important to recognize that there will be, along the way, a sense of negative energy that will try to resist us, disrupt us and distract us from being and living with God.

This negative energy will come in the form of causeless fears, depressions, lethargy, hopelessness, confusion, negative suggestions, resentments, angers, conflicts, sickness and a myriad of other ways. We can discern negative energy by the downward dragging pull that it exerts on us. Where the sense of God is always uplifting, elevating and joyful, negative energy always pulls us down.

Most people assume that these negative feelings and forces are just the way human life is. And for many that's the case, because there seems to be a numbing pall created by these negative feelings which hangs over the world and makes it difficult for the masses of people to rise above it.

But for the person who has sensed the energy of God, and wishes to live in this realm, the problem of negative energy becomes more acute. Negative energy actively resists these persons' attempts to stay close to God and to bring God's goodness and life into the world. And if these persons don't recognize the various gross and subtle forms of resistance that negative energy presents, then their lives will be filled with unnecessary pain and suffering.

Are we saying that negative energy is a force outside ourselves? I believe that it is. And though such a position might seem absurd to some people, I believe it must be said if only to alert those persons who are most susceptible to negative energy's influence.

LETITIA: And it's important that we see that negative energy is not just an inevitable or natural part of life, but that it's actively evil.

JOHN: That's right, because if we believe it to be natural, we're less apt to fight against it. We're more apt to acquiesce to negative energy, thinking that this is just the way things are—that there's nothing we can do about it. Which is not true. We can overcome this negative force if we're aware of it.

You know, we have often said that the joy is in the overcoming. When we have overcome any form of negative energy with God's energy then we find that we have emerged from our difficulty with an incredible, joyous sense of having accomplished with God. This creates a deepening with God that seldom happens in any other way.

There have probably been tens of thousands of people who have experienced God's love and who have wanted and wished that they could live forever with that love, but they didn't because they were obstructed and resisted by negative energy and never knew it.

CAROLINE: That's really true!

JOHN: God is not that difficult to experience and to live with. He is not holding Himself back from this world.

LETITIA: That's a beautiful point.

JOHN: But without recognizing negative energy and destroying it, we have little hope of experiencing God deeply or continuously.

CAROLINE: Negative energy remains hidden until you become aware of it. Now we've learned to recognize it. I think one of the most helpful things is to realize that all negative energy, such as depression and sickness and death, does not come from God.

JOHN: It's also helpful to realize that negative energy attacks our weaknesses. To be aware of our weaknesses is to be more able to guard ourselves against negative energy. For example, suppose we're prone to be anxious or sickly. Negative energy will try to come in through these doors. It would try to tell us our anxiousness is part of our personality. Or our sickliness is just our inevitable constitution. It would try to suggest a thousand different reasons for the way we think and feel. This is the way that negative energy keeps itself hidden. But once it's exposed as *not* part of our personality or *not* part of our constitution or *not* our own thoughts, then we have the chance to defeat it—to destroy and to overcome each onslaught of negative energy until it's destroyed for good.

LETITIA: The most aggressive way that negative energy has come in on me was with a sense of intense drowsiness for no reason. The drowsiness would come especially when I wanted to be close to God. A kind of numbing sense would come over me that would put me to sleep much of the time.

It was almost like the imagery presented in *The Wizard of Oz,* when Dorothy and her friends got into the field of poppies. They fell into a drugged state that put them all to sleep for hours. This is how negative energy has worked me. It wasn't a matter of having too little sleep. It was a kind of stupor. I use the word stupor because it describes the feeling of that staring state in which one can't focus on anything. This stupor pulls you down into its pit, and pretty soon one realizes it has nothing to do with sleepiness. Instead it's a state of fixation where one is unable to fully function. All forms of negative energy attempt to make us unable to function.

JOHN: I think you've stated it exactly. That staring, depressed, downward pulling state of stupor is the essence of negative energy. The accompaniments of this evil sense are worries, irritations, hatreds, resentments, sickness and an unending legion of fears. If this state of stupor is the root of negative energy, fear is the offshoot.

LETITIA: This brings to mind something that came to you, John, a few weeks ago. It had a big impact on us all because of the truth of your statement. You said that God is the attacker. God destroys all negative energy as we feel ourselves as part of God.

JOHN: Yes, as we feel ourselves part of God's power, then we begin to discover that we can attack and destroy any and all forms of negative energy. Before we had this power, negative energy—whether in the form of pain, sickness, anxiety or anything else—would back us down; would make us acquiesce; would make us feel like a victim. Now with God's power we stop backing down. Now we rise up with His energy to defeat and destroy negative energy as it occurs in our lives. What a joyful discovery that is.

Summing Up

JOHN: We've covered a lot of ground today. One of the things we talked about is that God can be found only when all our seeking and knowing has stopped.

We explained that feeling God's Spirit is our central emphasis. For without feeling God's energy, religion becomes a matter of creeds, doctrines and knowing *about* God rather than directly experiencing Him.

We pointed out that to feel God's energy continuously we must yield or let go of our lives, moment

37

by moment, to the sense of His Spirit. We must allow God's Spirit to guide us, protect us and bring us more fully into His Kingdom.

We said that to live continuously with God is a gift from God—one that He freely gives to all who desire Him sincerely and intently, and who are willing to relinquish the false sense of themselves for the reality of their true identity with Him.

We mentioned also that to live continuously with God we must begin to attack negative energy. Negative energy with its suggestions and sensations is the central reason that the seeker doesn't sense God continuously. Therefore, through the power of God's Spirit, this negative energy must be attacked and destroyed. Then God's energy and joy can be sensed in freedom and allowed to deepen and grow.

These are the things we discussed today. We hope with all our hearts that our conversation will help others. I know it has helped us to see more clearly the process of experiencing and living with Spirit.

CAROLINE: Yes, it really has.

LETITIA: One thing I was feeling as you were talking is that as we start to sense God we start to realize this is our real self. We begin to realize that in truth we are a part of God.

CAROLINE: That truth takes time to comprehend. It's a gentle teaching from our Father through the giving of His Spirit. Gradually it dawns that He really *is* our life.

JOHN: He's the only true life we have. Human life is ephemeral. His life is eternal. Therefore, as we're part of His life, we too are eternal.

CAROLINE: It's hard to remember my sense of life before I sensed God. And I don't want to. I don't think any of us wants to.

JOHN: Yes. We're less and less experiencing life humanly because we're continually experiencing God's life. This is the proof of the possibility of living with God now.

CAROLINE AND LETITIA: Beautiful . . .

II

Living With Spirit

JOHN: We talked the other day about how we could experience Spirit. And we briefly discussed how to live with Spirit. Perhaps now we could go more into depth about how we can live more fully and continuously with Spirit.

With all the problems each one of us faces, how do we keep that flame of Spirit alive? How do we bring that beautiful dimension of God's world into our world and apply it day by day? How do we live with it? Really live in that joy continuously? I think it's a question people who have experienced Spirit have seldom asked. I believe most people who have experienced Spirit consider that such experiences occur only rarely, or that these experiences happen only when one is in deep meditation. So they may never have questioned whether it's possible to live continuously with this beautiful sense of love and joy pulsating through them. Live this way in their daily lives, while talking to people, while walking, driving, working. While doing anything and everything.

So I feel if each one of us would explain how we

live with Spirit it might be helpful for others who
have similar desires.

The Importance of Desiring God

LETITIA: For me, the most important part of living
with Spirit is having a strong desire for God. This
desire is the main key to living continuously with
Spirit. For if I desire something other than God first,
then these other desires will keep me focused on them
and away from God.

Maintaining a strong desire is not always easy.
But without it we're not likely to yield to Spirit unless
we realize, perhaps only through memory, how beautiful Spirit is. Desire then will begin to return. This
is where prayer has helped me. I would pray to the
Father with the small degree of Spirit I still felt, asking
how I may yield more fully to Him. Within the
prayer I would begin to feel an inward release that
would allow God's Spirit to grow.

CAROLINE: When you're really down and not feeling
Spirit, you have only the memory of It. But this
memory doesn't contain the feeling of Spirit. So you
can only pray to feel Spirit again. I remember the
first time I prayed for the desire to feel Spirit. I was
feeling so low, so far from God that I couldn't really
care that much about being close to Him. So, I just
said, "Please help me, Father. I want to feel that
desire."

JOHN: As we're discussing desire, I'm questioning why some people have a strong desire for God while others don't. And I realize that this desire for God comes from feeling His Spirit. Without feeling His Spirit, to some degree, we simply can't truly desire Him.

We can desire to find a belief, creed or doctrine that's satisfying—that will perhaps remove some of our fears and insecurities—but we really can't desire Spirit.

So before we can desire God we must first feel His Spirit. And to feel His Spirit we must be somewhat open, sensitive, and aware. That is, we can't just live continuously within the hard shell of our egos and expect to feel God's love to any degree.

CAROLINE: Yes, and having felt Spirit, the sensitive and aware person is more susceptible to attacks by negative energy, which would try to take away or cover over this beautiful feeling of Spirit.

JOHN: Yes. As we've said for them the problem with negative energy is more severe.

How Negative Energy Works

CAROLINE: What one doesn't realize, until one has lived with Spirit for awhile, is that the human being is living in a false sense of life. We've come to call this "material consciousness." By this we mean that we live in states of despair, loneliness, depression, fear, hopelessness, sickness with times of happiness and contentment interspersed.

And we believe that this false negative consciousness is what life is really about—what our world is really about. Until we begin to realize that our real world and real life is with God, we can't live continuously with Spirit.

LETITIA: And through realizing our real life with God, we're able to identify negative energy.

CAROLINE: This negative consciousness seems to give us reasons for negative feelings. That makes them seem more logical and real.

JOHN: That's right. And from this so-called logic we give those feelings names, such as depression, arthritis, cancer, which only gives negative energy a power which it wouldn't have without the dreaded thoughts and images that accompany such naming.

CAROLINE: And we accept these names and images as true. I think that's where psychology feeds this consciousness. We're constantly asking, "Why do I feel this way? What is it?" That keeps us focused on the negative sense and away from God. I'm not against psychology. It's a useful tool to help many people live in this world. But it has nothing to do with living in God's world.

LETITIA: Isn't it amazing how senseless this negative energy is? It can produce such a despondent, low feeling and all the while it takes away our desire for anything but its depression.

JOHN: In its stronger forms negative energy seems almost like a spell. It draws you into that starey, lethargic state where you don't want to do anything. You don't even have enough human energy to attempt or want to get rid of it. As you've both said, at these times it covers up our desire for God which is the main fueling force that keeps us wanting to yield and to be with Spirit.

Jesus realized that unless you desire God more than your own life, it's impossible to enter the kingdom. Since feeling Spirit, we better understand this statement. Desire *is* the prime factor. But without beginning to destroy negative energy there's very little hope of maintaining a desire for Spirit.

LETITIA: The desire we feel for Spirit is not just a desire for Spirit to enhance our lives. It's the realization that Spirit can totally be our lives. And that's different.

CAROLINE: That's well said. I think one is tempted to listen to the suggestion of negative energy when it says, "You want to feel my life more than God's life." That's so easy to listen to before you're strong with Spirit. In fact it seems to govern your desires before you really realize that Spirit is your life. It takes awhile to understand these things. You sense something lovely but you don't realize yet that you can experience everything with Spirit.

The Energy of Love

JOHN: I remember, Caroline, after you first felt Spirit, you desired It with all your heart. Daily we talked about Spirit and how to keep It alive. And I know there were times of much interference.

CAROLINE: Yes, there really were. Each day I wondered whether I'd be able to feel Spirit. It was almost like we've said before, I was driven. I was just pushed into finding out what this feeling was.

I can remember calling you once, John, and saying, ''Help me to understand what this is about.'' Because I was feeling this tremendous energy of love and realized it was the first true thing I'd ever experienced.

JOHN: Love, yes. And Truth because It's absolute in Itself.

CAROLINE: And I could see you really heard that. It wasn't just somebody saying, ''Gee, that feels good, tell me more about this.'' But I think you realized then that Spirit was really alive within me. That the kindling had taken.

JOHN: That's right.

CAROLINE: Kindling, or coming to life, is how it felt. I desired this feeling with all my heart but it was a struggle at first to know how to feel it. So much of the time it seemed to be gone.

I used to go into the bedroom in the morning and sit by the window where the sun was coming in, and I would begin to feel this energy of love sometimes in my legs. It would start at my feet and come up into the area of the chest, and I would feel that when this feeling was there I was fully alive. God's life was fully with me.

I have since realized that Spirit doesn't have to be felt in the way that it first happened to me. I think God must bring His sense of life to us in the way we can best accept it.

JOHN: Yes.

CAROLINE: And after we have felt His energy, we must learn to allow it.

JOHN: "Allow" is the word you first gave us, Caroline.

CAROLINE: Yes, I mean if one feels Spirit a little, just start allowing more if you can and pray, "Please help me to keep allowing more of Your Spirit."

JOHN: Beautiful.

CAROLINE: It is.

JOHN: Someone is going to rejoice in that statement.

LETITIA: Yes, that's perfect.

JOHN: We're uncovering some aids which might help the person to begin to live with Spirit's energy.

CAROLINE: I've never expressed "allowing" that way. I never thought about how important it was to me.

LETITIA: I didn't understand at first about asking God to help me allow His energy to grow. What I used to do every morning was go down to the beach and sit on a little point of land. Then I would pray, asking God to guide me that day. During these prayers I would many times begin to feel Spirit. I don't believe I felt Spirit in the body the same way you did, Caroline. I would feel It more as joy and love which would uplift me through my day.

CAROLINE: I remember when I was first sensing Spirit how reading the four gospels would liven the energy within me. Because with Spirit I was really beginning to understand what Jesus was talking about. And as I read, the feeling of energy would grow stronger.

With this allowing of Spirit would come the feelings of joy and peace and love. Love mostly. It was almost like a current of love at times, circulating through my body. It was as if these feelings were a part of my body. I feel now, when I'm deep with Spirit, that my being is a part of God.

JOHN: It takes a certain sensitivity to feel this "current of love." It helps to be quiet to experience this love in the body. Many religious people ignore the body. We've found that God's love is felt in the body. Especially when one is in need of a healing.

CAROLINE AND LETITIA: Yes.

JOHN: But I think we should be careful in differentiating between body and mind. Because it's our whole being that's feeling Spirit, isn't it?

LETITIA: Yes. It seems that I felt myself as a part of something much bigger and more perfect than anything I, as Letitia, had ever felt. It was just an overwhelming sense of love.

JOHN: How did you know it wasn't just a heightened emotional state? That's often confused with God.

LETITIA: Emotions come from the human. There might have been emotions as a result, but that was only my reaction to this beautiful sense of love I was experiencing deeply for the first time. The experience itself was pure, unconnected with human emotions, and perfect. I somehow realized that at the time.

JOHN: We realize the emotions are a human mind product. But this love is a product of Spirit.

LETITIA: Yes.

JOHN: You weren't doing anything to generate the feeling of love.

LETITIA: No, I wasn't.

JOHN: I think it's important to state again that we are feeling an energy that we're not generating. In fact the energy is only felt as we yield ourselves and not when we project ourselves. It's a beautiful sense of love we couldn't possibly humanly produce. It comes from a Source totally outside ourselves.

CAROLINE: What comes to me, Letitia, is that you were feeling your whole being. Your true being. I feel this love when I walk the hills. It is simply love. I feel it along with joy and other beautiful feelings. But love, I think, is the essence of our being.

JOHN: I remember years ago I asked myself whether it was possible to live continuously with this beautiful sense of love that many times I felt. I just had to find out. For this sense of love was the only thing that gave my life meaning.

During the next several years I went through many frustrating times. I recall the many evenings while on a walk, or sitting before the fire at night, Spirit would be there with Its beautiful sense of lightness, love and joy. And then an extraneous thought. A telephone call. An interruption of some sort and It would be gone. What anguish I'd then go through. To have felt this energy of joy and love and then have it disappear. And all the ''spiritual techniques'' I'd learned did no good. Spirit couldn't be brought back by them. So the frustration just increased.

I'm so thankful that I no longer suffer that frustration—that Spirit is always with me now.

CAROLINE: As you talk, I realize the true gift that Letitia and I have been given. We haven't mentioned yet that in the process of feeling Spirit, or in our desiring to stay with Spirit, John could bring us beautiful help from God by directing this energy to us.

On the days that one falls, and there are many at first, you get discouraged. Hopelessness can set in. On these days we would give John a call and he would reinforce the Spirit within us by directing this energy of Spirit to us. To feel that kindling just suddenly coming back, one rejoices, "It's here again!"

JOHN: We've all felt that way.

LETITIA: Yes.

JOHN: When Spirit is sensed again what a joy that is. We start living again. For without sensing Spirit, we weren't living at all.

CAROLINE: That's right.

Helps We Have Found to Keep Close to Spirit

JOHN: What makes our connection with Spirit now easier to maintain?

LETITIA: As we become more familiar with how Spirit feels this enables us to yield more easily and continuously to Spirit's energy. Therefore, we're less vulnerable to negative energy and don't get backed down so easily every time we encounter it.

Another beautiful help along the way for me was keeping a personal journal. Every time I felt Spirit strongly I would record my feelings. Then in times when Spirit wasn't as strong, I would read about those moments when It had been. This kept me from the discouragement of negative thoughts. It was a kind of protection.

JOHN: You saw the truth in your own writings.

LETITIA: Yes, I saw the truth of Spirit in my journals. This brought about a renewed realization and feeling of God's energy.

CAROLINE: When I first started sensing Spirit I would make cassette tapes recording my experiencing of Spirit and the difficulties along the way. The first time I recorded I felt I had nothing to say. But when I played it back to myself I felt Spirit from my words, the same as you did from your writings, Letitia. It brought the feeling of Spirit back to life. That was a beautiful gift.

JOHN: Though the feeling of Spirit was tentative with you at first, Caroline, like a beautiful new flower, Spirit's realization grew within you. Today it's solid. The roots are very deep with both of you.

CAROLINE: I feel desire, prayer and allowing were the things that caused the roots to deepen. I know now that I was growing more than I realized.

JOHN: Yes.

CAROLINE: I think also that just experiencing Spirit over and over again each day finally breaks through the barrier of our physical life and you really see a spiritual life, or life of Spirit. This makes one more devoted to living with Spirit.

JOHN: Yes, we slowly begin to see the emergence of our new Spiritual identity, which creates a devotion to Spirit.

LETITIA: You can't help but be devoted.

CAROLINE: It's part of your being.

LETITIA: Yes.

CAROLINE: I think when Jesus said, "The Father seeks such to worship Him," the word "worship" is perhaps misinterpreted, because God gives one the sense of devotion that really is worship.

LETITIA: Beautiful.

JOHN: The energy of God's love *is* devotion because when you feel this energy it's so marvelous and joyous that it's all you want. Therefore it's not a matter of the person thinking he ought to be devoted, or should try to be devoted, or should discipline himself to become devoted. All he wants, after a while, is to be and live with God.

After I had felt God's love for a while, the love became so important that I didn't want to do anything without feeling Spirit's energy. Whether I was out on my walk, or writing, or engaged in business, or talking to people, or chopping wood for my evening fire, I'd seek to sense Spirit. Which meant I desired to be in a state of yielding to God.

My evenings were especially a delicious time with Spirit. After the day's activities I'd sit down before the fire for several hours before dinner and just melt into God's love. So many times I would feel my body totally filled by the power of God's energy. This is one of the most joyous times, for God's power is subduing the false sense of ourselves and bringing forth the full sense of our eternal being.

CAROLINE: Yes, we're all in the process of learning about our eternal life, and learning how to overcome the difficulties that keep us from it.

One difficulty is when I feel any kind of discomfort in my body. Or when my mind is working overtime trying to solve or cope with a problem. Then I find it's difficult to yield to Spirit. I may partially yield, partially feel God's life, but the mind and body keep interfering.

JOHN: Aren't the mind's separative thinking and the body's isolated sensations the only elements that make us feel ourselves separate from God? Feeling ourselves disconnected from God, we attempt to reconcile ourselves to Him through belief and faith, creeds and disciplines. Where the fact is if we learned how to die to this false sense of self which the mind and senses have created, then we would actually *feel* ourselves connected with God. Therefore no reconciliation through these other means would be necessary. And man's religions would change dramatically or become non-existent.

The problem is that negative energy creates in us a fear of letting go of this false sense of self. It creates the fear that if we do then we'll become a non-entity or fall into lethargy or lose our individuality which just isn't true.

On the contrary, when we have let go of the false sense of ourselves, we begin to discover we have a new identity—one that's part of God. And from this participation with God, we find we have a new energy which springs from the energy of God. And we have a real individuality based upon the intelligence, creativity, and love of God.

LETITIA: Oftentimes, for no apparent reason, negative energy will seem to create the feeling of a block or barrier to our letting go. We may greatly desire to let go to God, but still the feeling of resistance is there. In this case, through Spirit, we can recognize the feeling of a block or barrier and direct the energy against the feeling. Which breaks down this kind of block also.

JOHN: There are several things we have found to do when negative energy attempts to interfere. First, we can isolate the negative sense and direct Spirit's energy against it. For example, we can isolate the feeling of tiredness, or pain or any form of discomfort —get its quality and location into sharp focus—and then let go and channel the energy of Spirit right at the opposing feeling. Then, when Spirit's pure energy contacts the negative sensation, a state of leavening, removal or replacement of negative energy begins to occur.

It's interesting to note that many times as we're directing toward, we'll say, a pain in the body, that the realization occurs that God is right there where the pain seems to be. This realization is tremendously powerful in ridding ourselves of all physical and mental difficulties.

You know, directing is an entirely simple act. In

fact the simpler we keep it the more potent will be the results. Because it's the pure power and simplicity of God's energy that does the healing and replacement of negative energy, and not the complexity and complication of our human desires for a healing. Over and over we've come to realize this.

Another way we've found to deal with negative energy is through what I would call the "wheat and tares" method. This involves our realizing that pain, depression, fear—all forms of suffering—don't come from God. Therefore they can't be part of our real being. So we can let go of our suffering—I mean, just drop it like you'd drop a physical object. When we actually do this we begin to feel separate from the negative feeling. In essence we've divided ourselves from the "tares." And the beautiful thing is that after we have separated ourselves from the tares, these tares begin to wither away, because they no longer have the fuel of our fears, mulling and worrying to keep them alive. We can't fear them or mull them if they're really not part of ourselves. Therefore they must self-destruct.

Negative Energy's Effect on Creative People

LETITIA: In discussing the different ways of destroying negative energy, it makes me think of all the creative people past and present whose lives have been affected by negative energy. I wonder how much this aggressive negative energy kept them from living fully with Spirit? And how much their inspiration and works were affected by it?

JOHN: Certainly many creative people have felt the energy of God. To me, it's evident by their works. But most of those whom I've known and read about had extreme problems to face.

CAROLINE: Do you suppose that they had the wrong focus? Maybe they felt the energy but didn't realize it was from God. Therefore they didn't call upon God to help them keep it.

JOHN: I think that's right.

CAROLINE: The feeling or awareness of this energy can be taken away without help from God.

JOHN: Because they didn't realize it was from God, I believe, many of them lost their creativity and inspiration.

CAROLINE: You say, "Nature help me," and it can't help you. You say, "Love help me," and it can't. You say, "Muse, help me," and it can't.

LETITIA: Many of them may have thought that their genius allowed them to feel this creative energy. That this energy was generated by various levels of their minds, and not by a Source outside themselves. If they could have realized that this sense of creativity was not generated by their minds, they may have learned how this sense could give them greater life. And perhaps produce even greater works. Possibly many of these people felt that their creativity was sustained within their genius and knowledge. They probably didn't realize that the mind could not contain this creative energy.

CAROLINE: Perhaps they were trying to sustain it. That's probably why so many creative people sought solitude and closeness with nature, instead of realizing or understanding the source of their genius which may have been God. It would be so easy for negative energy to take away the sense of creativity from these people because they didn't realize what they were in touch with.

JOHN: I think what happens during moments of creativity is that one's being is open to Spirit's energy which *is* the creative Source.

Over the years I've read dozens of biographies of writers, musicians, artists, poets, and I would wonder why their lives so many times ended in shambles; why these creative persons, in touch with the Source, should be so neurotic, so angry, so depressed, so frustrated, so sickly. Now I see that negative energy especially attacks these people because they were in touch with the Source. And by being in touch, they were giving to the world some-thing uplifting, something beautiful, something that could inspire. And, as we've discovered, negative energy attempts to disrupt such "givers" from giving. This shouldn't make us fear it. Rather it should awaken us so that we can fight against it and over-come it.

CAROLINE: Because God's the one overcoming for us.

JOHN: Absolutely!

LETITIA: One reason that many people don't recog-nize negative energy is because they're afraid to be-lieve that something such as this could exist and harm them.

CAROLINE: It was the last thing that seemed possible to me. When I saw nature's beauty around me, I could never believe there was an evil force in the world. It wasn't until several months after I sensed Spirit that I began to wonder what was keeping me from having the beauty of Spirit all the time. It was only with my coming deeper and deeper into Spirit that I began to sense this opposing force. Finally, I realized it was the only sense that was keeping me from God's life. This is where the battle is.

JOHN AND LETITIA: Yes.

LETITIA: Also, many people probably have over-looked the possibility of negative energy, or evil re-sistance, because it's been personified as a devil.

CAROLINE: Yes. The concept of a devil can keep one from realizing that there's an actual force that resists God's sense of life. There's a belief that if you feel God, your troubles are over. And if you felt *only* God this would be true. But at this point we still feel negative energy and therefore have to deal with it.

JOHN: A serious encounter I had with negative energy happened a number of years ago. I was extremely sick. My overcoming of this sickness with God was not immediate. It took many months. But there was a gradual moving forward even though there were many days when I was brought down very low. But each time as I learned to trust God, He taught me how to better destroy the sensation of sickness. Because, as I've discovered through years of experience in dealing with sickness, that's really all sickness is, a sensation. And through directing the sense of God against the sensation of sickness, the sickness must recede and disappear.

The most difficult sense I had to overcome was that of a tingling, electrical feeling of numbness and exhaustion in my body. I found that every time that feeling would take me over the sickness worsened. So I prayed one day, somewhat out of desperation, and asked God to teach me how to defeat that sense. Over the months that followed I began to learn how to let go of my body and let God's energy flow through it. With this learning the numbness and exhaustion gradually receded. And the sickness lessened.

Negative Energy's Effect on Man, Nature and the Universe

LETITIA: From youth the human progresses into old age and death. As for nature, we see beauty disintegrating and being destroyed with time. This evolutionary process we look upon as nature's economy and basis for new life. But God's life doesn't contain death.

JOHN: Negative energy would contend that it has polluted all of nature with its poison. And its evidence is pretty convincing when we look about us and see man, the animals, the physical universe all being created and then destroyed. And from this evidence we theorize that God has some wondrous plan behind this creation-destruction process. But I don't think this is the truth at all. I believe this destruction process can be attributed solely to negative energy.

The other day I read about the recent space probes. On every planet within our solar system scientists have found an utterly hostile destructive environment. Venus, for example, the so-called love nest, has temperatures of 900 degrees and winds up to 400 m.p.h. Surely no God of peace and love could be responsible for that.

Also I'm reminded that the second law of thermodynamics—the highest known law of physics—states that everything in the universe, all the planets, solar systems, and galaxies, will eventually end up in chaos. I don't think a God of intelligence and order could possibly be responsible for that kind of universe. But many of us believe He is. So we're caught in the life-death-chaos syndrome. And from our belief in this syndrome we form our concepts about God. We make God into both a doer of good, and a doer of evil. Or if not a doer of evil, at least an allower.

So this, it seems to me, is what the battle's about —the destruction of negative energy as it occurs in our lives, and in the lives of others. And the questioning and uprooting of our existing beliefs about ourselves, the universe and God, which I feel can only be done intelligently after we have begun to sense God's energy.

The Relative Reality of Negative Energy

JOHN: We've been discussing negative energy at some length. And it's important that we do because it's the only barrier that keeps one from living fully with Spirit.

However, let's be careful that we're not making negative energy into a reality. The truth of the matter is that negative energy is only a reality to the human mind and senses. It's not a reality to God nor to our real identity with Him.

CAROLINE: As you come to realize that you're *only* God's child, from this standpoint negative energy doesn't exist.

LETITIA: Spirit shows us this in our deep times. When Spirit is all we feel, then negative energy doesn't exist. But we can't just start out saying that there isn't any evil. Because then we won't be able to effectively deal with its sensations.

CAROLINE: That's right. Spirit doesn't have the capacity to feel negative energy. Therefore, when we do, that tells us immediately that we're under attack.

JOHN: I'm reminded again how these many interferences have only helped us grow closer to God. That's the blessedness of living with God. No one likes to go through pain and suffering. But sooner or later each one of us does. So it's how we deal with our pain and suffering that matters. If we deal with it with God we're elevated right out of our problem and into God's incredibly beautiful world. And that's joy. Absolute joy. Our problems are just there to be overcome. To be transcended. Which may take persistence.

CAROLINE: Persistence is such a gift. You're constantly called on to feel God's energy, instead of lapsing back into the thought of what the problem seems to be.

JOHN: It seems like persistence and desire are tied together. For without desire for God one is not going to persist with God. I think of the persistence and desire Jesus had. He persistently stayed close to God through all his trials—in his deepest pain and sorrow. The desire for God continued all through his life. His life was devotion. Absolute devotion to God, in everything he did. Along with devotion was his absolute humility. He said, "Of myself I can do nothing." The realization of this truth is the essence of yielding, humility and healing.

CAROLINE: Yes.

JOHN: At every turn Jesus used the overcoming of his human problems to move more fully into God's kingdom.

CAROLINE: I was thinking about Jesus and how his total focus on God and desire for God kept him close to God's life. I wonder if some religious teachers by keeping focused on their desire to teach and to help may miss the central point of religion, which, I feel, is to sense God's Spirit. If they first sought to yield to God then they'd be able, to some extent, to let God do the teaching and helping through them.

I'm realizing there are two kinds of desire, and two kinds of love; there are two kinds of any feeling. God can give you His desire, His love, His joy. Or you can say, "I feel joy, I feel love, I feel desire," but they have nothing to do with God. Only the feelings that He gives you are the ones that give you true life. The feelings given by the world and the mind are also taken away by the world and the mind.

LETITIA: And as we've already said, Spirit is the desire. Is the love. Is the joy. Spirit consists of all these qualities.

CAROLINE: Yes.

JOHN: These attributes of joy, love, desire, and all the other beautiful qualities of life have reality in God. They come from God. They are not something that the human being can manufacture.

CAROLINE: Or even imagine.

JOHN: That's right. I think we have covered some ground.

CAROLINE: As much as we know so far.

III

The Benefits of Living With Spirit

JOHN: We've talked about how each of us first experienced Spirit. Then how this flame of Spirit is kept alive. Perhaps now we can discuss the benefits that Spirit brings to us and others as we live with God's love.

You know, God has shown us a whole different way of living—a way that relies on Him to manage our lives. We've found as we relinquish our hold on our lives, He brings us into the fullness of His life which is beyond all human imagining.

What a beautiful gift He's given us in the sensing of His Spirit. Within this sensing is all guidance and protection. All love and caring. This is a tremendous benefit.

Joy, The Primary Benefit

LETITIA: The first benefit I think of is the joy I feel from Spirit. I feel joy not only for myself, but I have learned to direct this joy to others so they can rejoice. This to me is one of the greatest benefits.

Sometimes it feels to me God rejoices with us in the sharing of His joy. It seems He's been sharing His joy with us forever, but we haven't been aware of it until now. To feel that joy and participate in His joy is ecstasy.

The fullness of God's joy is with me so much of the time. This joy is more than a benefit. It's a whole new life. The joy of Spirit replaced my fears, frustrations and pessimisms. These negative feelings gradually faded away as I began to realize I could trust God. And that trusting of God created a beautiful harmony in my life. This is joy.

JOHN: So the benefit *is* the joy.

LETITIA: And the alleviating of the many negatives which would keep us from God's joy.

CAROLINE: The beginning of feeling God's joy is the beginning of the alleviation of our human pain and suffering.

JOHN: The physical and mental pain that everyone suffers and that needs to be healed.

The Joy of Healing

CAROLINE: One of the most beautiful benefits which brings joy to ourselves and others is the healing of the physical and emotional ills all of us experience.

I remember especially one of the earliest healings.

It involved my daughter Katie. She called from New York one day to say she had a cyst and that the doctor wanted to operate. She asked, "Can you help me?"

John and I worked several weeks before Katie called to tell me what had happened. She said she had awakened one night terribly frightened. She knew at that moment that she didn't want her body to be cut open. She was terrified of having this operation and she called out, "I accept all help!" She felt that was the turning point.

On the morning of her final examination before surgery, Katie said she had this beautiful feeling come over her. "I don't know how to describe it except it was like a waterfall going through me. That's the closest I can come to it. And at that moment I felt cleansed. I knew I was healed! I knew I was all right!"

When the doctor examined her he said, "I just can't believe this. I've seen cysts go away. But I've never seen one this size disappear. I just can't believe it!" Katie says he mentions it every time he sees her.

JOHN: I remember later when she called me she said, "John, you should have seen the look on the doctor's face when he couldn't find the cyst. He was really befuddled."

I was very grateful for this healing. I felt it was important not only for Katie but for you, Caroline. Since it was one of your first healings, I wanted you to see that this energy really could heal.

CAROLINE: It was the first time I really realized the power of God. Since then so many beautiful healings have taken place.

JOHN: Yes, I remember the first major healing I was involved with years ago. It was with my dad. I got a call from Florida saying that he'd had a massive heart attack. The doctor referred to it as a heart explosion which is a terrible image to be presented with.

I immediately went to work with Spirit attempting to send some of the love I was feeling from God to him. At the time this was the only way I knew how to work. I remember all the way on the plane I kept working and praying that he might feel this love from Spirit. And as I did I was more able to break through the thoughts and images of his physical condition and feel more of his spiritual identity with God.

That night when I got to the hospital he was in intensive care, but evidently was feeling better for he recognized me and talked to me despite being heavily drugged.

The next morning when I met the doctor, he explained in vivid detail my father's problem. With each negative description the doctor presented me, I realized, from feeling Spirit, the total invalidity of such diagnosis. The doctor's diagnosis only pertained to my father's physicality and didn't consider his real being which lived and moved in Love. This is the truth that would heal his body. I remember thinking as we stood in the hospital corridor, "What a different world I'm experiencing right now than the world of sickness that the doctor's describing and that's all around me.''

Later in the morning the doctor again met with me. ''I've been looking at your father's x-rays and I just don't understand. Last night they showed he had massive heart damage. Now I can't find any evidence that he ever had a heart attack! I just don't understand it. It's the most amazing thing I've ever seen.''

Well you can imagine how I felt. I about jumped through the roof. It had worked! Though I didn't know exactly how. What I did know was I was working with the energy of Spirit. Still, I'd had serious doubts whether the energy could heal such a major problem.

But God showed me that working with Him would heal anything. This gave me a tremendous lift in confidence, and a better understanding of how healings were effected. Looking back, I see now that Spirit's energy broke through that numbing pall of fear and depression that always accompanies sickness. All sickness is within that pall of fear and depression. So if the healer can break through the person's fear then you have a healing. But one needs to work with the power of God to really be effective.

CAROLINE: Another special healing of a heart problem occurred with my friend Georgia. It was the first major healing I had ever worked for.

This beautiful lady, who was in her late seventies, was scheduled to have open heart surgery to replace a deteriorated heart valve. Her doctor had

69

run tests and had said that the valve was in such disrepair that an operation was her only hope. There was one test left to perform and that would be done when she went to the hospital.

Several days before Georgia was to go to the hospital, her daughter brought her over to talk about the possibility of receiving a healing from God. Georgia had heard that I had received a healing for my back and she wanted to see if anything could be done for her.

It was a most beautiful afternoon. As we talked I felt God's energy flowing through me in a steady stream of power. Georgia said she felt love filling the room. She put her hand on her chest and said, "I feel that I'm just filled with love."

As I talked to her about my healing from God, I just let the energy flow. And all the while I silently prayed to God asking Him to help Georgia and to guide me in what to say.

The next day I called John to tell him of the beautiful experience with Georgia. I asked if he would work for her too. A while later he called me to say he felt the healing had already taken place.

JOHN: I'll never forget the first time I met Georgia. It was a few days after we'd begun working for her. Her face was all aglow. She just radiated with love and joy. I remember how her eyes were filled with a trust in God—trust in a God she had always believed in and whose love she was now feeling.

The witness she gave to us that day was magnificent. She said that all she wanted to do with her life from now on was to help bring this sense of God to others in need. She said that she knew she was healed even though the doctors had yet to confirm this.

CAROLINE: She was so totally filled with love and joy she couldn't help but have been healed.

Several days after our meeting, Georgia went to the hospital to have her final test. She said when the doctor came to explain the results of the tests he looked happy but puzzled. He said, "I don't know how to explain this to you because I don't know what has happened myself, but your heart valve has been miraculously restored. There's no need for an operation!"

Georgia's healing has brought such joy to all of us. As Letitia has said, the first benefit is the joy—the endless strength and joy of Spirit.

JOHN: Absolutely.

CAROLINE: At first you want it because you feel so much better. And then your life with Spirit opens up more and more beautifully into countless benefits which we'll probably talk about.

JOHN: Within the energy is the joy. Because it's untouched by anything negative.

CAROLINE: Yes, you can't experience Spirit without joy. This is an absolute quality of Spirit. Human joy is perishable—always with the threat of leaving. But

God's joy of Spirit is not perishable. We have to learn to yield ourselves to this sense of joy. It's a continual process of yielding.

JOHN: Yes.

CAROLINE: And in this yielding we receive God's love, too. Love is a large part of what God gives as a benefit. Because in this energy you are walking love.

LETITIA: When you feel yourself as walking love, you're functioning from perfection. Someone could look at you and say you're living in the world like everyone else. But, really, you're living from the perfection of love.

JOHN: That's when you know beyond all doubt that you're part of the love that God is feeling in Himself.

Union Through God With All Nature

LETITIA: This morning as I was thinking about the benefits of Spirit, I looked out into the ocean and saw a seal. The joy of God rushed through me when I realized I was truly enjoying the sight of the seal with the energy of God's love. Because of the fullness of love there were no interfering thoughts or agitations. A sense of timelessness was all around. And in a gentle, beautiful way I felt in union with the seal through this love. This timeless union with nature happens quite often now because I can view things with that love.

JOHN: I remember years ago when I first walked the hills around my home, I was constantly looking toward nature to trigger the feelings of peace and harmony within. This constantly frustrated me. For as I looked out at those beautiful hills and the magnificent ocean and clear blue skies, I felt nature was so much more peaceful and harmonious than I was feeling.

Today this has all changed. Now I realize how much more peaceful and harmonious the feeling of God inside is, than the hills, sea, clouds and trees. Now I know I can bring something of love and harmony and eternalness to nature. And what a benefit that is—to share God's love with nature.

CAROLINE: God gives us the ability to share with all that's about us, whether it be people or nature. It seems He rejoices in the giving of His love and joy. Consequently, life is a celebration every day.

JOHN: A long time ago a friend said to me, "There's something you've found that brings joy to your life." I replied, "Yes, I can't explain it. It's just a joyous sense I feel inside for no apparent reason."

Ever since childhood I've felt this joy. For years I didn't relate it to God. Matter of fact, I was quite adamant about not relating it to God. But now I realize that the Source of this joy is God Himself. It's the essence of God's Spirit. And this joy is for everyone. Jesus said that anyone who thirsted could drink from this well of joy and life. And yet so few of us do. This is why the world is filled with so much unhappiness.

Helping Others With God's Energy

LETITIA: The beauty of this energy is that it can be directed against this unhappiness. And when it is one of two things happens; either a person is changed by it to the degree that their whole life turns about, or they simply are relieved of the cause of their unhappiness.

What a beautiful gift to be able to give someone God's healing love and joy. Most people want to help others, especially when disaster strikes. But seldom do people know how to help. We've been given a tool that will always help. For the first time in our lives we can say, "Yes, we can help." This is one of the greatest benefits of Spirit.

CAROLINE: Yes.

LETITIA: To touch the world with God's Spirit is our major purpose now. And what a wonderful purpose. What a joy-filled work.

CAROLINE: We've come to realize that when we're helping someone our real responsibility is to let go and yield to God's energy. The healings come from God's energy. His love. Not from ourselves.

JOHN: I remember when I was first learning to heal with the energy. I was trying to combat the sense of sickness that I was feeling. One particular evening I was really feeling bad. Negative energy was whaling away with that tingling numbness and general sense of exhaustion which I've already described. Feeling I was losing the battle, I called out to God and said, "Father, I need more of Your power to fight off these sensations. Show me how to receive it."

Within moments the words formed, "If you want more of My power you must get more out of the way." This answer was so logical and obvious that I wondered why I hadn't thought of it before. Now I realize that the haze and confusion negative energy puts around one obscures even the most evident solutions to problems.

Since that evening, if I feel lacking in the power of God when working for others or myself, then I recall that lesson and get more out of the way. This is bound to increase our sensing of God's power and the power of our work.

Other Healings

JOHN: We've described healings we've had by denial and directing. A healing I'll never forget came about through faith.

I was called home one day from work because my daughter, Shanna, was having a bad asthma attack. When I got there she looked very bad. She was gasping for air and was very frightened.

I sat down on the bed and took her hand. "Shanna," I said, "Do you know that God loves

75

you? And that He's going to heal you?'' For several moments she just looked at me through those glazed eyes. Then, without saying a word, she turned on her side and closed her eyes. Gradually her breathing became easier. I stayed with her until she had fallen fast asleep.

When she awoke she was healed! Since that day, years ago, she's never had another attack. Although I worked for her, I think the major reason for her healing was the faith she had in God.

When I asked her about this recently, she said that she felt it was her faith in God that brought the healing. ''When you told me that God loved me and that He'd heal me I knew it was true,'' she said.

To me, this is a perfect illustration of what Jesus said about faith making a person whole.

LETITIA: Faith can be an extremely important element in healing. It aids in releasing one's fears. Then the healing energy of God can be felt.

JOHN: If the person in need can't seem to release his fears, then it's up to the healer to help through prayer, denial and directing.

You know, as I look back on the many healings we've had, I think of how the energy has healed cancer, lung tumors, encephalitis, bursitis, colitis, arthritis, torn ligaments, not to mention the colds, flus and other minor ailments.

CAROLINE: And there have been emotional healings too. Tremendous emotional healings of deep depressions. And we've had healings for financial needs.

JOHN: Yes. A financial healing recently for a friend of ours was remarkable. She went from extreme need one day into financial sufficiency the next. It was an incredible healing.

CAROLINE: When we stop worrying and start praying and are willing to take action as God leads us to act, then it becomes a constant participation with God in every problem that arises.

LETITIA: And everything that God's energy touches is the beginning of a healing. When we bring God's harmony to the world, it brings a healing.

CAROLINE: Yes.

LETITIA: I had a healing recently for a situation with my little house. I had just moved in and was so excited to be given such a beautiful gift. Within weeks, though, it was threatened to be taken away from me. Through prayer, the fear of losing my home quickly passed and I felt confident that God was going to bring me His answer to this problem. And He did. I ended up keeping the house. It was a big lesson about total trust.

JOHN: I saw you let go of the problem. You released it almost immediately through prayer. You had learned not to hold on to these negative possibilities which are just temptations to believe that harmonious situations can become disharmonious.

God worked out your problem with the house perfectly for everyone involved. That's why it's important that we keep out of the way after we've prayed for a solution to a problem, because we don't know what's best for us. God does. But we don't. We can't.

LETITIA: Because the human is limited in his understanding of how the perfect solution can come about.

CAROLINE: I was realizing the other day that as we live here with Spirit we are God's life on earth. And God is going to live in harmony and perfection. That's the only way He can live.

JOHN: His harmony came through again recently for you, didn't it, Caroline?

CAROLINE: It surely did. All my life I've had problems finding enough money to pay my bills. I had been worried for years about this problem. Now, living with Spirit, I wanted to handle that problem. So I began praying to God asking Him to show me more of His life and sufficiency.

A few days after I'd been praying a man came to my door and asked if I would like to sell my house. That opened my mind to the idea of receiving money through the sale of my property. I called a real estate man and he came over and appraised the house. To my total surprise the value was over twice what I had expected!

LETITIA: The real healing was the gift of feeling that God was providing all that you needed, wasn't it? When we feel God's Spirit, It begins to replace our fears.

JOHN: It seems God's indicating, in effect, that His wholeness and harmony are going to be, because that's all there really is. It's important not to block it. Then it will come through.

As you know, I had a similar healing as yours, Caroline. Years ago a large company threatened to throw my partner and me into bankruptcy. There seemed to be no solution to our dilemma. It was the darkest of dark times for me. I had a family to support. I had dozens of financial obligations to meet. And here, within ten days, I was faced with losing everything I owned.

So I really began to release the problem to Spirit, for there was nothing else I could do. And that's when I began to feel and know beyond all fear and doubt that God somehow was going to solve this "unsolvable" dilemma.

I remember when I'd talk to my partner back east, I'd find myself saying, "Don't worry. Things are going to work out." When he'd ask, "How?" I'd reply that I didn't know how. But I could feel with Spirit that they would. Somehow my calmness and sureness helped calm and assure him, even though I know, at times, he thought I was a little naive.

God did work out the problem. Not immediately, but step by step. And our creditors, seeing that we were going to make it, went along with us until they were paid.

After God brought me through that potential disaster, I've always known that He would take care of me. Not only financially, but in every way.

CAROLINE: That's what's happening to me now. It feels like a huge healing. Just immense. And because of this healing other situations in my life are being touched. I know what God can do now. And I can trust Him to take care of my life.

Benefits From Long-Term Healings

LETITIA: When one goes through these long-term healings it feels like there will be no end. But with God it will always work out. That's not to say that it'll always be easy. But, truly, we move through these situations untouched. We really do find ourselves at the other end of the whole problem and often don't fully realize how we got there.

JOHN: We get to the other end of the problem because God takes us there if we allow Him to. Which means we must constantly remember to work for the problem and then let go of it.

I recall that one day as I was walking along the street to my car in Santa Barbara and feeling very sick, the thought struck me that I was going to die. I'd been fighting the sense of disease for many months and had recently felt I was losing ground.

At that moment of realizing that I was going to die, I felt a total internal release of all effort to save myself. Where for months I had been struggling to survive, I now gave up all my human striving and said, "Father, if I'm going to live I need Your help." Almost immediately, I felt the last bit of resistance within my body let go. And then a great inrushing of God's energy occurred which instantly began to combat the many symptoms that had been hounding me for so long. I knew at that moment that instead of dying I was going to defeat this sense of sickness and live!

That day in Santa Barbara God gave me even a greater gift than the destruction of my illness. He gave me a constancy of His Spirit that I had never had before. Ever since that day I've never been without Spirit's energy. There are times when it's not as full. But it's always there.

LETITIA: In a longer healing such as yours, John, God teaches us so much. The teachings are part of the healing. There is so much spiritual growth we might need. So much learning to live with God's love. When the healing takes time we benefit so much.

Many times we realize what God is giving us during the healing process. Other times we must look back to see the many benefits we've received.

CAROLINE: One of the things you learn is that if you stay with Spirit, yield to It, then the healing is going to come even if you don't think there's any improvement, at the time.

LETITIA: Actually, this yielding is important not only during a healing but constantly as we're learning to live with Spirit.

One morning when I was sitting on a hilltop struggling to be with Spirit, I looked up and saw a

hawk soaring in the sky above me. The realization
came from watching it that I wasn't allowing Spirit
to take control and come through me. I hadn't been
yielding my all to Spirit as this hawk had totally
yielded to the wind. This realization released me to
Spirit.

Spirit's Energy Dissolves Thought

JOHN: One of the main interferences to our releasing
to Spirit is thought. You know, this false sense of
consciousness—the human consciousness—thrives
on ideas and images, dreams and desires, fears and
worries. Its life is thought. It can't act unless thought
is first consulted. Thought is its god, the ruler of its
life. The content of this false consciousness *is* thought.
Without thought the walls of its house collapse.

What a trivial, tiring thing is thought as com-
pared to the considerings, insights and comprehension of Spirit. But to live without thought is not
so easily accomplished, for negative energy perpet-
ually feeds our human minds with thoughts of
pleasure. Thoughts to fear. Thoughts to keep us
embroiled in our conflicts.

As we've said, many religious teachers have
seen the culprit of man's conflicts to be thought.
But no one I know has shown us an effective way
to deal with thought, because I don't think there is
a human way! I believe only the energy of God can
deal with thought effectively. And it deals with it by

dissolving thought and replacing thought with a clarity and awareness that needs no thinking to comprehend or to act.

I realize how much I used to think. How much I used to stew and worry about problems. Now the energy burns away most thought and replaces it with an expansive comprehension that's guided by Spirit Itself. What a benefit that is!

It seems to me that the central difference between thinking about a problem and considering a problem with Spirit is that thinking is a totally isolated act. It's not connected to a creative Source. Thinking is based upon conditioning, experiences, traditions, opinions, ideas, beliefs, hearsay—all those things that the human mind has collected consciously, subconsciously and unconsciously.

On the other hand, awareness or considering emanating from the energy of Spirit *is* connected to the creative and harmonious source of God. Therefore the decisions, actions and solutions coming from such an awareness will be creative and totally harmonious.

LETITIA: Every time I hear these isolated, self-conscious thoughts, I've begun to realize that they're trying to draw me away from Spirit. I recognize them as coming from a source apart from God.

Before, self-conscious thinking governed my life. Now, for the most part, God's sense of Spirit guides me. More and more I'm relying on God and not on my ability to think and plan out my life. When we recognize, from Spirit, our lack of human ability, we naturally let Spirit be our ability. Reliance on God's energy really works and brings about perfect solutions.

CAROLINE: I believe what we're describing is the difference between thinking and being. For example, when I feel God's energy of love and then I sit down at the typewriter to write, I'm participating with God. I'm participating with Him in His clarity, comprehension and creativity. This makes me a better writer. But mainly it makes me more of a being than a human could ever imagine.

LETITIA: Absolutely. That's true individuality.

JOHN: I once heard a religious teacher say, "Thought creates the thinker." That is, thought creates the image of a self-conscious human being with his world of problems. Therefore, this teacher maintains, for the human being's problems to end thought must stop. So again we're back to doing something with the mind—making an effort to stop thought. Where if we'd yield the mind then there'd be no effort involved. We'd be doing nothing with or to the mind. And through yielding we might begin to feel the energy of Spirit which eventually would dissolve thought. With the energy there's no need for self-conscious thinking. Without the energy one has no other recourse than to think self-consciously.

The other day an elderly man said to me, "The thing that worries me so much as I get older is that I'm not going to be able to think. That I'm going to lose my mind and become senile." And I understand that. This is a major fear as one gets older.

LETITIA: Loss of memory and the ability to think is a major worry for the elderly.

JOHN: The worry is over the losing of the acuteness and activity of the thinking mechanism. This certainly should be a concern. But what will keep the mechanism alive, active and alert? I believe only the energy of God's Spirit will. For everything It touches, It improves, heals and enlivens. And with the energy touching us we're enlivened, active and alert in an entirely different way.

LETITIA: Human thought and knowledge can't begin to compare to the perfect intelligence of Spirit.

JOHN: That's right.

LETITIA: I know many people have said things that have far exceeded their human knowledge, and then wondered, "Where did that come from?" I think they've experienced this intelligence, without thought, from time to time, when self-consciousness has been dropped. But when living with God's Spirit continuously, one becomes aware that many things said come from that Source of intelligence rather than thought.

CAROLINE: This kind of intelligence and clarity of Spirit has no connection with the human mind.

LETITIA: These understandings and insights don't come from thought but from Spirit.

JOHN: And they're not dependent on the person's age, education or experience.

CAROLINE: One of the beautiful benefits is that Spirit has no age. Even though our ages are different this has never caused us any problem in relating to each other in Spirit.

JOHN: You know, the dissolving of thought by Spirit also brings a great sense of peace. I recorded in my journal one time as I sat before the fire alone, "I wonder if anyone has ever experienced the total sense of peace that I feel now?" Then I went on to say how, at that moment, God's life and energy had enveloped me totally—so much that all desire for anything else left me. I was just totally at peace with this sense of life. What a benefit that is.

LETITIA: The stopping of time.

JOHN: Yes. The stopping of time, which happens when thought has been burned away by the flames of Spirit. This is peace.

LETITIA: It is. Spirit is where the stopping of time exists.

Thy Kingdom Come In Earth

JOHN: One of the things we're learning is how to bring the Father's kingdom onto this earth. The Father's kingdom is an energy or life that is whole and perfect. But how do we bring His whole and perfect life into contact with the inadequacies and imperfections of this world?

For years I struggled with this question. I'd look out my window, day in day out, feeling God's life and wondering how this life could touch or penetrate matter—the trees, the birds, animals, people—so that the disease, decay and destruction I saw all about would diminish.

It was during my healing that the puzzle began to be solved. I started to realize that matter, physicalness, was simply a sensation. Therefore, I saw the possibility of God's world touching this world. That is, God's sense of Spirit touching and penetrating the sensations of matter or physicality.

The healing of my illness by the *sense* of Spirit was living proof, for me, that the two worlds could touch. But it took directing the energy into the place where the sensation of sickness was. Likewise, it took directing of the energy into the place where matter or physicality was. In other words, into the body or human senses. And as I did this for others, many people were not only receiving healings but they were also feeling the energy of Spirit touching their bodies. And by feeling the energy they started to realize that there really was a different realm of life that was filled with goodness, beauty and love. Now we could relate to each other on an entirely different basis. We could begin to relate through the common love we were feeling from God.

Often times, when I'm involved in healing, I

think of Jesus' words, "If I cast out devils by the Spirit of God, then the kingdom of God is come unto you."

LETITIA: This truly is healing with the Spirit of God.

JOHN: And it's learning how to bring Spirit to others and ourselves. This is bringing the kingdom of God to earth.

CAROLINE: We were talking awhile ago, John, about the time you said, "I can't live another day without Your help, God." And how the healing touched your body and changed the feeling of your body, and brought the truth of your life with Spirit. I was realizing this could be an endless process of being resurrected right here on earth.

We've had both physical and emotional healings. They were both healed in the same way by Spirit and bring the same feeling of our Father's life. The same could be true for a healing of the sensation that the body dies. In a way it's the same thing. This ends the sensation of death.

JOHN: What you're saying may seem outlandish to some people, but this realization is born from constantly being with Spirit. When we're immersed in Spirit's sense of eternal life we see there's no reason to die. We see that death is just a false concept or sense contained within the structure of a false consciousness. So if that false sense of consciousness is destroyed while we're here on earth and replaced by the sense of Spirit's life which is our real being, then, of course, we can't die. Death will have been overcome.

LETITIA: Everything with God is out to rebuild us. Give us new birth . . . New life . . . Everything.

Living a Transformed Life

JOHN: This energy is really a different realm. A different sense of life. To a great extent we live a timeless life.

We know what it means to live a self-conscious, self-willed, time-filled life. We know the sensing of that self-conscious energy with its frustrations, worries and efforts "to become." Now, having relinquished that life, a different sense of life and energy fills us. And as we learn to keep self out of the way God's energy is with us constantly. To me that is the final answer to life—to actually live life with God.

LETITIA: This is the complete benefit.

CAROLINE: Yes.

JOHN: To have a different Source of life. To live a different life—a transformed life. Transformed because we're participating with God's life.

LETITIA: And everything around us, our whole living environment, becomes transformed. Love controls our lives—where we live, how we live, where

we work and the kind of work we do. Just everything in our lives eventually falls under the guidance
of this love.

CAROLINE: Love brings about the perfect environment for Spirit to grow. All I have to do now is
allow the Father's life—His sense of Spirit—to be
with me and I'm taken care of.

JOHN: And it's effortless. This is another benefit
isn't it? We don't have to exert the least ounce of
effort to be with Spirit. We have learned not to
exert effort, because when we do the feeling of Spirit
diminishes.

CAROLINE: It's not that you don't work. It's a different kind of work. The work is in yielding continuously to Spirit. And then doing the Father's
work using His energy and love.

This yielding brings you into the realization
that you're God's child. The beauty that you are
His child of Spirit.

Summary

JOHN: At the beginning of our conversation today
we discussed the benefit of joy—the benefit of actually
sharing in God's joy through our participation with
the energy of His Spirit.

As I looked through my journals today I found,
not surprisingly, that joy was the central theme.

The joy that we feel with the Father is the essence or main benefit of participating with God's Spirit. And out of this joy, found in the energy, come healings for ourselves and others. Out of this joy comes the sense of sufficiency that God will always care and provide for us. More than sufficiency, we are truly rich—rich with a joy and love that the world cannot know, because it comes from God. It is of God. It is only with God.

One of the greatest benefits for me has been to see how God has brought about a fullness of Spirit within both of you. I have seen how your lives have been literally transformed. I have seen how your devotion to God and His work has grown. I have seen your healing work become more powerful. I have seen all aspects of your lives become more harmonious.

And through seeing these things in you, the realization has deepened in me that Spirit is really practical. Spirit is really true. Spirit's energy can really overcome all our problems in this world. This is a tremendous joy and benefit.

Letitia: God's Spirit is this joy. We feel His joy, and then direct this joy to others. It's a perfect cycle of love and joy that comes from the Father and returns to the Father. And we're all feeling it. It's what Jesus said, "As the Father hath loved me, so have I loved you." Also he said, "Love one another." That's the perfect cycle. All the benefits stem from the Father and are given to further His kingdom. And it truly is happening.

CAROLINE: Yes, it is.

JOHN: I wrote down a little prayer I found in one of my journals that's in line with what you're saying, Letitia. It reads, "My Father, you are my first love always. For the love I feel from You has given me life, joy, health and sufficiency. You, Father, have given me everything."

That little prayer is precisely how I feel about the benefits of living in the kingdom of God.

CAROLINE AND LETITIA: Thank You, Father.

Silence

AMEN